DELUGE

ALSO BY LEILA CHATTI

Tunsiya/Amrikiya

Ebb

LEILA CHATTI

DELUGE

COPPER CANYON PRESS

PORT TOWNSEND, WASHINGTON

Cover art: Sedira Zineb, *Self Portraits or The Virgin Mary,* 2000. Copyright Sedira Zineb. All rights reserved, ARS, New York / DACS, London / Artimage 2019. Image courtesy of kamel mennour, Paris.

Copper Canyon Press is in residence at Fort Worden State Park in Port Townsend, Washington, under the auspices of Centrum. Centrum is a gathering place for artists and creative thinkers from around the world, students of all ages and backgrounds, and audiences seeking extraordinary cultural enrichment.

LIBRARY OF CONGRESS CATALOGING-IN-PUBLICATION DATA

Names: Chatti, Leila, 1990– author.
Title: Deluge / Leila Chatti.
Description: Port Townsend, Washington : Copper Canyon Press, [2020] |
Identifiers: LCCN 2019056173 | ISBN 9781556595899 (paperback)
Subjects: LCGFT: Poetry.
Classification: LCC PS3603.H37978 D45 2020 | DDC 811/.6—dc23
LC record available at https://lccn.loc.gov/2019056173

98765432

COPPER CANYON PRESS

Post Office Box 271
Port Townsend, Washington 98368

www.coppercanyonpress.org

Poems in this book have been published in the following journals:

The American Poetry Review—"Haemorrhoissa," "Tumor"

Beloit Poetry Journal—"Intake Form"

Boulevard— "Annunciation (My body now a chamber)"

CALYX Journal—"Mary in the Waiting Room at the Gynecologist's Office"

The Cincinnati Review—"God's Will"

fields—"Postdiluvian," "The Scare"

Four Way Review—"MRI"

The Georgia Review—"Annunciation (I have come to accept the story)," "Questions
      Directed toward the Idea of Mary"

Gulf Coast—"The Blood," "Night Ghazal"

Indiana Review—"Immaculate or Otherwise"

The Journal—"Etiology," "Odalisque"

Kenyon Review Online—"Angel"

The Los Angeles Review—"Nulligravida Nocturne," "Watershed"

Los Angeles Review of Books—"Haemorrhoissa's Menarche," "Mary Speaks"

The Massachusetts Review—"Still Life with Hemorrhage"

Mid-American Review—"Deluge (And so it was)"

Narrative—"Exegesis," "Landscape with Bleeding Woman," "Sainte-Baume"

New England Review—"Portrait of the Illness as Nightmare"

Ninth Letter—"Prayer"

Pleiades—"Litany While Reading Scripture in the Gynecologic Oncology Waiting Room"

Ploughshares—"Confession"

Poetry Northwest—"Metrorrhagia"

Prairie Schooner—"Eyes Opened, as Gods"

Rattle—"14, Sunday School, 3 Days Late," "Morning"

The Rumpus—"Annunciation (at the bedside)"

Smartish Pace—"The Handsome Young Doctor, Who Is Very Concerned"

32 Poems—"Morcellation," "Waking after the Surgery"

Tin House—"Sarcoma"

Tin House Online—"Testimony"

Virginia Quarterly Review—"Menorrhagia," "Mother," "Mubtadiyah," "Storm"

West Branch—"Annunciation (All night I leak a shadow)"

Willow Springs—"Myomectomy"

"14, Sunday School, 3 Days Late" also appeared in the anthology *Annunciation* (Phoenicia Publishing, 2015); "Immaculate or Otherwise" and "Morcellation" were included in the *Orison Anthology* for 2017 and 2019, respectively; "Confession" appeared in the anthology *Halal If You Hear Me* (Haymarket Books, 2019).

for Patricia

CONTENTS

♦

♦

From the depths I have cried out to you, O Lord

DELUGE

CONFESSION

Oh, I wish I had died before this and was in oblivion, forgotten.

Mary giving birth, the Holy Qur'an

Truth be told, I like Mary a little better
when I imagine her like this, crouched
and cursing, a boy-God pushing on
her cervix (I like remembering
she had a cervix, her body ordinary
and so like mine), girl-sweat lacing
rivulets like veins in the sand,
her small hands on her knees
not doves but hands, gripping,
a palm pressed to her spine, fronds
whispering like voyeurs overhead—
(oh Mary, like a God, I too take pleasure
in knowing you were not all
holy, that ache could undo you
like a knot)—and, suffering,
I admire this girl who cared
for a moment not about God
or His plans but her own
distinct life, this fiercer Mary who'd disappear
if it saved her, who'd howl *to Hell*
with salvation if it meant this pain,
the blessed adolescent who squatted
indignant in a desert, bearing His child
like a secret she never wanted to hear.

MUBTADIYAH

(Arabic) beginner; one who sees blood for the first time.

And indeed, appointed over you are keepers, Noble and recording;
They know whatever you do.

the Holy Qur'an, 82:10–12

Hidden in a dim stall as the muezzin called
all worshippers to prayer, I touched privately
the indelible stain. And watched, with a nascent sense
of kinship, the women washing
through the interstice of the door,
their veils slipping off like water, water
spotting their clothes like rain.
I thought the thought only
children and the pious believe, that I was, just
like that, no longer
a girl: the blood my summons, blot like a seal, a scarlet membership
card slid from my innermost pocket. I was newly twelve and wise
enough to be frightened. I had read the Book and so understood
my own was now opening, alighting
onto my shoulders like some ethereal bird flapping
briefly immaculate
wings, and understood, too, that I myself engendered
the ink with which, on its pages, my sins would forever be
written (not literally, but
this was how I imagined it, metaphor, as the blood brought
God's recorders like sharks to me,
menarche a bright flare, a matador's crimson cape)
—I had not been good
all my life but until this first vermilion drip
I lived unobserved, my sins not sins

because no one looked. And now,
above like a lamp suddenly
ablaze, God's reproachful
eye turned my way, a searchlight eternally
searching, and seeing and seeing—
I was as good as I would ever be. In the dark, the ruddy
iris stared back at me.

INTAKE FORM

Doubled for six hours and bleeding, I decide to go to the hospital
only when my boyfriend says *How long? Jesus Christ*—then puts me in the car, drives to the hospital.

Rate your pain from 0 to 10, 0 being impossible, the impassible
God, 10 being Christ pinned like a monarch, who was unlike all others wounded, who did not die to save you
in your version of the story, who endured the suffering of the world and everyone in it and never once
asked to go to the hospital.

Seven pains, or the pain sevenfold—pain like the pain of the Blessed
Mother in the desert, of the first mother who passed it on like an inheritance, of my mother—her first—
on her back, wailing, in this hospital.

How much blood, would you say? What's your best estimate, would you say? Would you say it comes constant
or in waves? You stayed in the tub, did you say? Did it soak a tampon, did you say? How many tampons, would
you say? How quickly, would you say? Is this abnormal, would you say? Is this a lot of blood for you,
would you say? Is there any chance you're pregnant, would you say? Is it possible this is your period,
would you say? When was your last period, would you say? Say, is that your boyfriend, I'm going to ask
him some questions, okay? I'm just going to ask him some questions about your bleeding, okay? Just
clear some things up, okay? Get a clear picture, okay? Then we'll get you into the hospital.

In the twenty-second year of my life, in the twelfth month, on the fifteenth day of the month,
all the fountains of the great deep burst forth, and the windows of the heavens were opened.
 And I caught heaven in a plastic bag. Heaven teeming steadily into a bag beneath my jeans.
And—God forgive me—I think *mulberries*. And an angel speaks the measured, anodynic
language of angels directly to my vein. And I bob in and out of what divulges no horizon. A
voice above pronouncing *flood* and me affirming *yes, a flood*. And so, one day, I'll say it was—the
word came down to me so simply that first day of the spate, of the hospital.

DELUGE

And they were oblivious, until the flood came and swept them all away.

Matthew 24:39

And so it was—twenty-two and suddenly

gushing, as if a dam had burst or a thundercloud
deep inside the storm of me, the flood
like a horse loosed from its stable, blood

racing down my thighs, I thought
surely I will die, so much of me
outside of me and still more

leaving, an exodus, the blood
rushing as animals do just before
the worst of it, as they must have

done before the deluge came, those left
behind, as from their homes
the unspared—perhaps one of them

a woman, my age—looked on
with something close to wonder,
unaware of what approached.

MARY IN THE WAITING ROOM AT THE GYNECOLOGIST'S OFFICE

She flips the silken page of a *Cosmo*
and sucks on her teeth. I watch

her immaculate hands as she scans
sex tips and checks again her phone.

Her veil hangs loosely, ornaments
her shoulders like a fresh drift of snow.

It's just us two. Across the room,
a watercooler gurgles beneath framed diagrams

nailed to the wall: uterus, fallopian tubes,
a vagina opening its deep

throated rose. Mary presses
her palm to the heat

of her breast, turns to me and says,
as if apologizing, *I'm a little nervous.*

Carefully she smooths
her blue skirt, glances

at the ceiling. Whispers,
One was enough.

In my hand, an empty cup.
Mary crosses

her legs, fingers the slender
chain around her neck.

She rubs her thumb against
the pendant's tiny face, his miniature

arms permanently splayed.

MRI

I wear a gown that ties in the back; this is how
I am sure I am sick. The nurse can't be more
than a few years older than I, smiling
as if we're friends while I grip closed
the gape of my frock. Lying down
on the narrow carriage, I think
it's a bit like a grotesque sleepover,
me in my nightdress and the nurse
telling jokes, fetching me a blanket
to throw over my knees. I think
these things because I am young
enough to have slumber parties,
still young enough to feel entitled
to ease. And the nurse waves
to a technician behind the glass—a boy,
I mean a man—who coolly asks
what I'd like to listen to, the way a boy does
on a date, scanning the car radio,
or at a party where he knows everyone
will sing along, but I say *nothing*
as I slide in, arms by my sides
as if I were slipping into the sleeve of a sleeping bag
and it were simply my friends whispering
in the next room, trying not to disturb me.

ANNUNCIATION

at the bedside   robed

      in white a white   blaze

  above

      a hum   of light

         like a supernal

language   a dove in the dark

    bell of my thresh

         -old pain

pealing   like a Sun

   -day the attending

         announcing

    shadow

      widening   the dove's

  steely

beak *a bit*

 of pressure a sharp

  pinch

      in view on the screen

       apparitions

        black halos black

   seas void

 of boats

    or divinity

they are speaking now they are trying their best

  to appear

    human

    so I won't

startle   leave   but what

    they have to tell me

I don't want
to receive
the Word only
incarnate

once it slipped in her

sleeve

MARY SPEAKS

And what could I say when he entered, rude
as a dream, bare flame of a man with wings and demands

not his own? I'd been raised, a good
girl, to house

my tongue in my mouth, to be hospitable
toward strangers, suspicious of

no one. Perhaps I'd have been
better off

to be wary, but I'd been waiting so long
to hear God speak—I hadn't thought to think

of what he might tell me.

WATERSHED

The moment was, to the observer (my boyfriend,
and God I suppose, as He is always
watching and we were
otherwise alone), ordinary—February waiting for us outside
settled as a marriage, all dull
secular light and tepid weather, inside the room
a pale green, muted and slightly cool as if under the surface
of a pond, I emerged
from the bathroom still shedding
blood like water, still leaking like a tap, I had changed
into a paper gown, baby blue, with little bows
knotted along my spine, my body spiraled
back, ungainly, distracted, to hold
closed where I was exposed—he said
the nurse left something for me
on the exam table, a couple of white sheets
at the edge, I sank
onto blue plush, the stirrups
gaping to my left and right like two silver mouths,
and then those words, you know, I lifted them
so casually—

SARCOMA

When the doctor says the word *sarcoma,* I consider how it might be a nice name for a daughter, that good feminine *a,* the way parents name their children for all sorts of inappropriate things—apples, for instance, or the place where the baby was conceived—and I trace my fingers over the barrow of my belly as he speaks, flesh distended beneath the blue tissue I wear for a dress—an ideal grief frock, throwaway—and he says something about life expectancy but of course I expect my life, so plain I thought nothing would ever take it, and while he explains I cup my palms around my center—as if comforting a child, or covering her ears.

LITANY WHILE READING SCRIPTURE IN THE GYNECOLOGIC ONCOLOGY WAITING ROOM

And God said, *let there be blood*

And God said, *flood*

And God said, *good*

is a woman with fruit

in her womb and not

in her hand

And God said, *sin*

And God did not say, *forgive*

And God said, *I will make a stormy wind*

And God said, *son,* a breath

stirring

And God said, *highly favored*

And God said, *condemned*

And God said, *I will blot out man*

whom I have created, for I am sorry

that I have made them

And God said, *listen*

and sank a boy

in her like a stone

MENORRHAGIA

Christmas, flew home packaged like a gift. Beneath my jeans a childlike padding. Came to adore the wee god, his dolorous mother. All while bleeding like a can of cherries. Clots sluicing down my thighs. The storefront windows glaucous, spotted with ashen, ineffectual stars. From heaven dropped unrelenting sleet. The dawns all too bright and immaculate. Lit by snowlight, ached prostrate before a mirror, bare and quivering in its stare. The runnels running downward, red ribbons. Porcelain like a bank of snow. Each night a night silent and wholly unbearable. Stains blooming on sheets like poinsettias. Percocets tumbling like flurries on the tongue. *Fall on your knees.* Collapsed sudden in a vestibule. *O hear the angel voices.* Rose fevered, soaked with slush. Flew home for Christmas, plane niveous as a dove. The window's bleed hole haloed, a nimbus of tinselly frost. Leaned feebly against the pane. The cities rutilant, scarred by streets. The lakes spattered black and viscous. The sky blushing as if shamed.

MOTHER

If you had asked me, thirteen, what I wanted
to be one day, I wouldn't have said it.
I wanted, for a long time, to be anything
but myself, knew that a soon-to-be
woman was the second worst thing
in the world after a woman, full
stop, and I was heading there fast.
I could see it, my breasts rudely
nudging into view, their snug caps
like the knit caps of infants, rosy-
colored as a tongue. And how
terrifying, the thought of a mouth there,
rooting, and what could be drawn
from me that I didn't need—what else
skulked in me unseen, stirring in secret
vats with milk yet untapped, and blood,
the strange, new wellspring? I was just beginning
to understand the possibilities, my body's
elusive, independent workings, machineries
chugging away in dark chambers
not just *left to* but simply
their own devices, unknowable and sovereign.
What I wanted, always, to be:
in control. And I knew this was
impossible, just as I knew, even then, that
to be a mother was to be the only
permissible form of a woman, the begrudging
exception to the rule of our worth-
lessness.

So if you asked me again,
twenty-three, I'd tell you the worst thing

you could be is not a woman but
barren, the industry shut down and the parts
missing, malformed. And I'd tell you the shame of it:
the feminine failure, its ache
a reminder—at the center the tumor
ballooning, like hope.

On the scan a monochrome nimbus of indiscernible material—my own, of course, but its intentions opaque, its mouth not a mouth but a zero, a cipher, a space indicating a question it will not ask of itself, it requires me like a child to do another thing I'd rather not, to speak on its behalf, to determine its name so I might call it by it, so I might be accurate in my address, this precise knowing something like tenderness, my obsessive attention an ersatz love, and I cannot turn away from it, it resembles, too, I think, a fruit if fruit were buried, of my center, blank eye staring from benthic depths, and while I'm at it a chthonic pomegranate, a Pompeian fig cocooned or else the dark countenance of the moon, one of its seas, or the orphan planet of the dead, motherless stone, God of No and Never.

PORTRAIT OF THE ILLNESS AS NIGHTMARE

No matter how many times you ring the bell in the bad dark,
no one will let you in. You face the fun

house with its mirrors on the outside
so everyone can see. And everyone looks. You are in your underwear

and the room is cold. The doctor's stethoscope pressed to you
becomes suddenly a snake. Your heart hisses in its cage. Your heart sputters,

a doused flame. You are drowning in your blue paper gown, which recedes
in the back like an ocean, your skin a bank of hot sand.

The horizon bleeds and the days and you
wander lost in a city of scalpels where everything glitters

and pills fade like moons on your tongue. You sidle through
sterile labyrinths and piss in a cup. You wait in a room like a chapel

or the belly of a beast. Either way, you think
something will save you, you believe this the whole fearsome time.

Your god comes and he is ordinary and terrible. He confers
with the doctors at your kitchen table and tells you to eat

your clots, round as peas. You want dessert. You want to
deceive him, but he, like you, has eyes, and uses them.

You are grounded, in the ground. The pit is a tub
and you are washing in your body's black water. You rise

like a fever. You writhe on a bed on a stage, the strings reaching
toward heaven. There is a momentary break for everyone

else: intermission. They chatter in the lobby. You babble
symptoms in a white confessional. You fall from a great height and land

on a gurney. You are at the front of a classroom and you are stripped
to your bones. The doctor points to your pelvis. You model

the tumors—in this light they look pretty, like jewels.

ANGEL

After a month of asking, suddenly, a voice. It says *you deserve that which has happened to you.*
It says *I see what you do with your long, terrene hands.* Maundering through the banalities
of my life, it follows, speaking, as if from a frosty bag of peas in the freezer aisle, speaking,
while I am on my knees, scrubbing the bathroom floor, trying to love a man. Its speech is
disquieting company, but company nonetheless—a TV left on and turned low. It desperately
wants my attention but is polite, which is its defining weakness. Sometimes I catch it stirring
out of the corner of my eye—a glint at the end of my cat's whiskers, a spangle on the ceiling
of indiscernible source. More often, though, it looks like me, only a little off, like my
reflection in the pregnant belly of a spoon. In fact, when I speak to it, I use my own name.
I'm not sure if it minds. It repeats instead its refrain. It says *God has plans for you.* It says
I didn't say they were good.

HAEMORRHOISSA'S MENARCHE

I wanted to be a woman
until I was. What opened

in me brought such pain
I believed finally

one day I would die. But it subsided—
for a while. I remember thinking

I was cured, I could go back
to being a child.

Then the next month: red
seed in the morning's bowl

unfurling as it touched the water.

ETIOLOGY

they said it—you will   bring ██ upon your father you will bring ██ upon your family

      I was 13 I was in love when with him I felt   so much
      ██ when he said I could hurt you   so easily I said good

I deserved it I didn't know   how to stop I knew
    ██ followed me   like a strange dog   into the house

    but   I loved
      love that wasn't   obligatory   I wanted to

       be sure   someone   could
I was ██-filled I was ██less I sang Genie   in a Bottle I moved   my hips

       I wore my skin where everyone could   see it

EYES OPENED, AS GODS

and ye shall be as gods, knowing

Like suns I could not lower
my gaze from.
I admit I liked

the warmth of them—tongues
in the dark
of my ears like secrets,

palms
splayed upon
my thighs like stars.

God, I felt you
had designed them purposefully
for me,

as you had once forged
my foremother.
Felt a tug

of primordial
hunger. Dreamt of snakes
that let me

hold them. All day eyed
the shiny apples
of their throats—

14, SUNDAY SCHOOL, 3 DAYS LATE

I'm not stupid—
I know how it works.

But there was a time when
she was just some virgin nobody, too,

small purse of her womb
and her ordinary eggs

waiting like loose pearls.

THE SCARE

One year before I knew
I was sick, I was twenty-one
and one week late, I squatted over
a stick bought down the street
from my first apartment, my first
live-in boyfriend stationed in the doorway
gnawing at his cuticles, both of us
nodding, dazed, as I wiped away
piss from my shaking hands, saying
if yes, then yes, meaning *okay* and being okay
with it, waiting and waiting and only realizing after
the apparition—*no*—we might have been
half hoping for it,

                    and so,
a year later, when I am sick and squatting and feel
something slip from me
so big, I scream—(I am sure I have lost
an unbearable thing)—
but when he runs in to find me
howling, hysterical,
in the bowl there is nothing
but blood, a gelatinous clot
enormous enough to fill it, my body
throbbing, me wailing *Oh God, Oh*

                   God, I thought it was—
my face in my hands as the hour
passed slowly and I
waited, emptying, still something
like empty.

NIGHT GHAZAL

I boil night on the stove; soak it until it's thoroughly done, black.
We drink it like tea, unspeaking—swallow its moths, distant suns, black.

Through the telescope's silver barrel, litter of white stars
already dead. They glitter like shrapnel. The sky, gun black.

The blood comes and comes; I spend all night in the tub,
water running. It pours from me: gush of child undone. Black.

I tell him, *fill my darkest places.* My fingers grip too hard,
leave small moons along his back. The bruises come, black.

Dream, small death. I become a phantom above the bed.
Sleep, the simpler twin. The same eyes closing. The same gone black.

HYMEN

Second blood—I never knew you.
After the first, scoured the bed
for your blazoned blot, and came up
empty. Perhaps I was born without
you—a box with no prize
inside, a sundae
with no cherry on top. God of good
girls, god of matrimony, *mother-*
state, which I consider
a distant country with a discordant
tongue, did you speak
with God and conclude I hadn't
use for you? Once I was small
as your kin, so small
and for such a long time, longer than
I've lived, I fit inside my mother
when she fit inside her mother, and so on and so
forth, and further, a nest of matrons, *mise en*
abyme in which to be female is to be something
like infinity, and was it determined then
what kind of woman I would be?
It seems I've always been frightened,
little veil, of wedlock's
lock clicking shut. The heritable procession
of women whispering in the aisle
of my pulse *don't do, don't do, don't.*
And I haven't done, this
the gravamen, the grave
I've dug with the spade of pleasure.
                              But, wanting

seal of want, I did

want it, did choose to commit
my life's greatest transgression
with a benevolent accomplice, and so,
in the herebefore, you could say I am among
the spared. What a mess this messlessness
of you could have been in any
number of lives my size, billowing specters
of dresses on a line
of possibility, lives in which I am the brides-
maid, and you, maidenhead, the bride
given away, where I am the acquired
property and you the red ribbon
severed in the threshold, I
the purse and you the coin
tendered. Perhaps no one
ever told you, precious emblem
of innocence, simulacrum for
honor, that some believe
you the most important part of me, vital, like a heart
a man gets the thrill of bursting
where he can see it, that blood
is owed to him—and that's the heart
of it, isn't it? Of a woman, you
the only blood worth anything.

THE BLOOD

She had the blood, too. Bathtubs filled
to enameled lip and her body
pouring. As a girl, I thought being
a woman meant your life spilling from you
like a cup of juice you kept knocking over.
I was young enough to think anything
that bled was a wound. The moon
waited like a round-faced witness
in the window each month, steam
erasing the mirrors and the walls
weeping. All night the tap running
and running. I wanted to know
how pain made a woman
curl like a pill bug poked with a stick.
I wanted to know everything about suffering
so I could avoid it. I was young enough
to think things like that, seven years
small, when calamity was skinned knees and little
brothers and an upturned sundae
crashing to the floor like a chandelier.
All I knew of disaster was Hollywood
movies where houses were swallowed
easy as bubblegum and spaceships
hovered like gnats out of reach—ruin always
at a distance—and you could press your face into
your mother and everything would be all right
once you turned on the lights.
Sometimes, now, when the ache comes
and I am coiled in dark water, I remember
that distant self like a daughter
I gave up or lost in a bustling
food court and never saw again,

the remembering painful.
And sometimes I wonder if she knew
why her blood came angrier
than any other's, blood like my blood,
which now seethes and conspires and appears
on MRI scans like a black eye or a crop circle
or the earth's eager void.

METRORRHAGIA

Clouds purpling, clotted near heaven. Henrik says
the sky will burst, will be good for the seeds. Henrik
on his knees, planting, thumb turning in black

soil. Birds scattering, spotting the dark. My hands
at the faucet's mouth. Summer blackberries bleed
a strong stain. My black thumbs, turning.

Henrik on his knees, good to me. Plants
kisses on my cheek, holds my waist. My hands
turning a bowl clean. Purpling at the window,

clouds like blackberries, clots. Rain spotting
black soil like a stain, good for the seeds.
Cloudbursts sudden as a faucet. The sky's mouth

full with blackbirds like seeds. My body
stained, high above the knee. Dark spots
at the bottom of a bowl. Henrik planting blackberries

on my tongue, leaning into me. My hands
at my body's mouth, sudden. Heaven bleeds
brief rain. Clouds scattering, like seeds. Henrik's

mouth purpled with sweet. Sky darkening,
turning. My body floating, cloud-like, adrift
in clean water. A black stain spreading, like wings.

STILL LIFE WITH HEMORRHAGE

A wine crate for a nightstand, and on it, a rose
gone bad in a cup. Its water

a swallow of shadow, murk of rot
and sugar. Clothes sloughed, bodiless, and half-

eaten on a plate,
a plum in its juice. At the center

of the scene: a woman on a mattress
on the floor. Her arms cast out

as if preparing to fly
or as if pinned, savior

or specimen. Still asleep.
Day breaking through the window

a warm leak.
The woman in its spotlight

like a halo. As if something holy,
or at least chosen.

HAEMORRHOISSA

Did she, like me, lose years of nights,
up at an ungodly hour, washing the sheets? She must have been

very tired. She must have been ashamed, waking again
to a stain in the bed, still warm like a lover just risen, dayspring

seeping over the weedy yard outside. She likely had once
a husband, but not long, not after. Because no one touched her

she must have touched herself, she must have known a woman could
die from living untouched and preferred to be satisfied. Her red hands

turning slowly and brightly like fish under a faucet
in the back of the quiet, lonesome house. Sometimes, I'm sure, she thought

her life was all right. She ate, when available, the foods
she liked best, and moved her chair while reading

to the sunniest spot. She presumably prayed for some time, then decided to move on
to more fruitful endeavors, like grooming her eyebrows, or organizing the kitchen drawer,

always a mess. I'm sure she enjoyed a good joke. Occasionally had trouble
with self-esteem, generosity. She was the kind to need and need, like me,

endlessly. So when one day that god walked by, all boyish good
looks and not looking her way, she didn't, for a moment, hesitate, she did

what I couldn't do—a miracle within reach, she took it.

IMMACULATE OR OTHERWISE

Though I'm not trying, I am
disappointed. Mary did nothing
and God grew like a seed. I fuck men
and receive the punctual mess.
Always they think I should be grateful
for the stain like a petal pressed
between my legs, think this a miracle
against their clumsiness, the wilted
condom leaking in the dark.
There's a reason, my halfhearted
mantra against all that dejects
me: the first tumor budding
in the uterine wall, then the second,
the relentless deluge of blood.
My days persist conceptionless,
immaculate or otherwise.
I find success in determinable things.
But still, the sting remains:
my body one unchosen, vessel
of illness and ache. Call it irrational
prayer of the secular heart, progenitive urge,
but there's a reason, I know, why
I cry His name in the dark.

GOD'S WILL

When a child latches in the hollow
of a woman like a leech,

it is Your will.

And, too, when the body fails
and leaks like bad fruit,

it is Your will.

Once, you were clear
with your intentions, you left

no room for dispute—

your voice coming
through to Mary

like a snake through black water—

now, nightly, my ear
toward heaven

a cup catching shadows.

If Your word is Your will
and Your will is all,

collude with me.

TESTIMONY

There is a god, and there is no God but Him.

He has many names and answers to none.

On the Day of Judgment I will be called by my name and by the name of my father.

My name the dark I was forged in.

Dark which rehearses its return while I sleep.

Indeed, one day I will return to God, as it is to Him that I belong.

Indeed, this was part of the Message, and the Message was received.

I do not speak for God and He does not speak to me.

This an (arrangement/estrangement).

When asked my religion I answer *surrender.*

I pray with my head to the floor, with my hands where He can see them, with both eyes closed.

All this for Paradise, which lies at the feet of mothers.

Beneath my feet the temporal earth.

Which darkens where I stand.

PRAYER

until the blood surged I knew it only

as song Your word a piteousness

of doves pouring from my throat Your word

an asp whispering through shadow to more

shadow it was easy I learned early how

to beg and ask nothing I thought pleading

was the point I fell diurnal like a sun

to my knees I prostrated to distance

myself from smoke I yearned for

Your attention I did not comprehend

what was said *of those who have evoked*

Your anger or of those who are

astray each time I intoned *so be it*

ZINA

(1) Verily, it was heaven.

(3) allow me (2) I couldn't be certain You would

(5) so I sought my own (4) admission

(6) in the body

(7) of a man.

(9) You, my Lord. (8) Verily, I mistook him for

(11) God, (10) I invoked another

(12) I invoked an other.

(15) I proffered myself, (14) I prostrated— (13) Before him

(17) And pleasure (16) an oblation.

(19) angels (18) chorused through me,

(20) or an exaltation

(22) And each part (21) aroused from sleep.

(24) knew itself (23) named

(26) and stamped its feet (25) and bucked

(27) in praise.

(28) And the beast I was was

(29) glad.

(30) Verily, a woman, the first

(31) night of nights

(32) I required a man's flesh to come

(33) alive—

(36) I was afflated (35) his mouth grazed (34) everywhere

(38) he touched me (37) and each time he touched me

(40) anew (39) as though making me

(41) with his own two merciful hands.

46

NULLIGRAVIDA NOCTURNE

And they ask you about menstruation. Say, "It is
harm, so keep away from wives during menstruation.
And do not approach them until they are pure."

the Holy Qur'an, 2:222

He touches me.
Reaches across our mattress

on the floor like a raft, adrift in night's black
gulf. Headlights glide over the opposite wall.

Gilded. Quick. His hands
cresting the waves of my hips.

In the dark, I leak
more darkness. Inside,

an endless well. I know
now, deep within myself, myself

as harmed. Know deeper
the man I love

will never harm me. He's no god
but good

to me. Like blood, the night
comes and comes and

comes. I was taught
for years a touch like this

was fruitless, a sin
to love when love couldn't

root as proof. His
hands on my hips despite,

moored. If asked,
I'd make the trade—give up the inconceivable

heaven for a warmth
I can sense, the faithless

man who draws toward me
through shadow, knowing

who I am, what I can't be.

MORNING

I take the last grapefruit from the bowl and hold it
to know its weight. The doctor told me
the tumor has grown, is now this size. In my hands,
it feels conquerable, rind giving in to the press
of my thumb, pliable and sweet. A miniature
dimpled sun. I cleave it open and begin
plucking out its seeds. Beside me, a waiting
cup, an empty bowl. I watch as they fill slowly,
cradle morning's flush of light.

ANNUNCIATION

All night I leak a shadow
from the place I first learned shame.

All night the milky curve of the moon
pressed to the window like an ear.

God, I know you are
there, you are everywhere.

And yet you fixed her
in a shaft of light

and sent a man
who would not touch her, frightened

though she was.
You were there in the room

as you are here in the room
and the dark through

which I beseech you.
The man beside me

slumbers messageless,
unwinged. All night I listen

for you listening. If there
is something you need

to tell me, God, you must
tell it to me

yourself.

THE HANDSOME YOUNG DOCTOR, WHO IS VERY CONCERNED

The handsome young doctor, who is very concerned
with the future possibility of my body
in a bikini, insists

morcellation—a tiny bicorned prong
inserted through
a minuscule slit in my belly. *You'll barely see it*

he says, grinning
as though I'm already convinced. I imagine
the tumor minced, the blade a dervish

spinning. I say *I've read
this is dangerous.* He says, impassive, *of course,
everything has risks.*

Already checking the time on his wrist.

MORCELLATION

from the French

Less   invasive

the doctor says.   *To break into*   *pieces.*

Little morsels,   little slits

(for me) to come out of

(myself).   *Mon corps*—

my body—   a corpse,

a mis-   translation.   As I keep mistaking

blood   for *song,*   God

as something   owed to me.

               But the tumor lacks   language

               and so, in this way, is

infallible, and so   a little

                               like God. And, like God,

the terror is in knowing

               it could be   malignant, could be

               everywhere and all

                               at once.

LANDSCAPE WITH BLEEDING WOMAN

after Simon Jordaens's Christ Healing the Bleeding Woman

The clouds' batting overhead
like a gauze-swaddled seam, dirty cotton.

I see nothing as it is anymore; since

remembering my body as temporary, I impose it
anywhere it fits.

Could the trees be
trees, or are they stitches
suturing mud to heaven?

In a landscape I consider
first what interests me, the living
beings, which I identify as
those that bleed. There, interrupting

the skin of a field—sheep and shadow and one

woman on her knees.
I won't be the last

to look into a painting
like a mirror, to ignore
the glutted world in order
to better scrutinize the self. Is that me

crouched at the feet
of a god?

Of course it's not.
But say it was—untouched, He turns

away from me.

ODALISQUE (POLAROID TAKEN ONE DAY BEFORE THE SURGERY)

Look, I said.
That is the point.

Or, I said nothing. My lips
ornamental.

Or, my eyes spoke.
Or as good as spoke, agape

as two black maws
entering the conversation.

This is clear: my eyes looking
to ensure

you are looking.
Focus, I am

subject, supine in a bed
of white linens, pillows—I am framed within

the frame by a window
so white the world is

effaced.
Yet I remain,

I am limned
by its absence, and here

you are, with me, looking. (You want
the particulars; I deny you

the particulars.)
The scene, lacking

distraction, concedes me inordinate
importance, this is how

I see myself,
and how I wish to be seen—

but my body has
its own demands.

Does it silence or enliven
your desire, the reminder

I will one day die?
(This the question my body asks.)

ANNUNCIATION

I have come to accept the story of my own
obedience—how I waited not knowing
I was waiting, ear obliging, body
poised. You sent a man I could not
look at fully, or touch, he was a flame
which spoke, and I could not
be afraid—as it's told,
I rose instinctive as a dove
startled into flight, blue
veil fluttering
floorward and tongue
unglued—*may it be done*
to me I said, and it was done
so quickly, I thought to say it
meant I had some say, but it was
preordained—the breath
barely out of my body
before my mind had changed.

MYOMECTOMY

At the center of the dark
room an aureole: there,
pricked at the wrists
by IV cords, robed except for
the waist, my body
lay reposed and bleeding
like the inverse of the child-
God, my body left
open like a window.
They entered, innominate
doctors, their hands blue
as sky slipping through that oculus
to retrieve what had taken root—

it resembled a pomegranate
when lifted into view, ruddy
globe cradled by two hands, fruit
of the dead—but it was not
dead, nor was I, I was still
living, that bright vermilion
my proof—and so, like me,
they split my womb
right down the middle, the wound
precise. And from beneath
the tumor emerged, eager, as if to be
born—bald creature with no father
and no future. Savior of no one.

WAKING AFTER THE SURGERY

And just like that, I was whole again,

seam like a drawing of an eyelid closed,
gauze resting atop it like a bed

of snow laid quietly in the night
while I was somewhere or something

else, not quite dead but nearly, freer,
my self unlatched for a while as if it were

a dog I had simply released from its leash
or a balloon slipped loose from my grip

in a room with a low ceiling, my life
bouncing back within reach, my life

bounding toward me when called.

POSTDILUVIAN

And it was not done at once. And ache gyred like a dove unable to land. I was adrift in pain; I floated in and out and could not see beyond it. I thought it was the new world in which I would learn to live. But in a moment of clarity, the window, its curtains parted starkly like a tempest. Outside the pane, the actual world revealed. Houses, copses, lives of strangers flotsam doused in shadow. A sanguine glow soaking back into the earth. And what was left of it drained slowly from the room.

REMISSION

Because I cannot stand

       he carries me: lifts me from the bed as though I might
be further injured by his touch, or as if afraid it might be painful

       for him to touch me. In my bathroom's glow, his shadow or an Orans, before him
I raise my hands; it is the hardest thing I have done all day. Pain, and the shame

       of pain, and the pain of shame—he slides the night-
gown over my head and I am bared, livid

       from the waist down as if vestured in an ultramarine
slip, the umbilical catheter strapped to my thigh by elastic

       like a garter, cicatrix stitched across my abdomen taut
red thread, fraught with my own refractory

               blood—I weep when he sees and does not turn away

       from me. A freshet of fresh shame: not to be beheld by him but to be
held, gently, dipped backward into the shower's stream, everywhere his body touches mine

       darkening as if wounded—touched like this
after so long, so readily, I was convinced his love an affliction, my one

       transgression. Wished, having known it, never
to have known it. And, knowing this, and without a vow to bind him to me,

       he rinses my hair. Sits with me in the tub
like a boat at the center of a world with no one in it, where what will be

       done is already done and there is no need anymore
for forgiveness. A long time like this. And when

       I try to speak, from overhead water rushes
to fill my mouth, softly shushing.

AND IT WAS SAID

Unable to move, I am lying in bed. The milky March light
        diffused like mist, at once everywhere
though I did not notice it

filtering in. The phone pitched between ear
        and bare shoulder. My body
cut open in the neat and deliberate way.

I place my hands over the wound, though I am sure
        it's still there. The doctor's voice
sudden in the empty room like the voice of God. Everything

white and stark as the conception
        of a miracle: The many pills. The pain.
The duvet slinking from the mattress

like spume receding, revealing blue
        thighs, white wrappings.
In my one-bedroom apartment,

colorless and closed in
        as a dream, I receive at last
the word: *benign*—

        did you hear me?

ANNUNCIATION

My body now   a chamber   I have

closed off   to you. Sealed   my mouth, my hands

above the fiery   wound. Dark   the dark of

heaven, bleeding   in. So   quiet

I am sure   you do not   address me.

In my room,   the sudden   coruscation

only white   blades   of headlights

slicing through   the blinds. Still,   I looked toward

that brief   brightness. Injured   though

I was   by you,   for a moment

lifted   my gaze,   hoped—

STORM

The summer after, a storm
split the sky over Hergla and I wanted to be in it.
I climbed the rickety ladder to the roof where the night was
purple and vast and you could see
the whole bruise of the ocean. I was still
in pain, I thought I would always be in pain,
but it had receded like a tide and so
was bearable, almost welcome,
made me feel more acutely
alive. The clouds swelled violet,
violent. The gales battered me with sand.
For a moment, this seemed all
there was—as far as I could see the world
desert and ocean and heaven
shattering along its bright scars—
and I thought the creeping thought
of someone who has just made it through
her worst imaginable thing, that I must begin
imagining again for surely
a worse calamity awaits
to take its place, wondered if
I would spend the rest of my God-given-
back life bracing for the next
inescapable disaster, the earth or my body
cleaved right under me, the sky
falling in black drops like stones,
and though I felt this real fear the storm didn't subside
as it might in a movie of my life, suddenly
waning to prove a point—no, it kept on
in its wild terror, me there stunned
at the center, fixed as the ocean broke and broke

against the shore's skin, as the desert
raged on, barren and hissing.

EXEGESIS

I bled. God didn't
want to hear about it. He said *unclean*
and so it was. He said *it is
harm,* and so it was.

Want to hear about it? He said *unclean.*
Once a woman wanted, so he did
her harm. And so it was
first conceived: a woman suffering

because a woman wanted. So he said
cursed. And then he said *blessed*—
the woman chose to suffer, conceived
a god, though she never knew a man.

And God knows best. If He calls a curse a blessing
then so it is. And he said she was
clean—she never knew a man. I've known men but never a god
that bled and lived. But I did.

QUESTIONS DIRECTED TOWARD THE IDEA OF MARY

Was it the voice you feared, or its shadow?

Did you long for His touch or was suffering enough for you

      to know He was there?

Do you resent me my juvenile hungers?

Do you wish for me the freedom of a vast, barren plain?

What would you have done with your body if your body obliged?

Did it please you, your son risen at the end like a question?

Do you pity the angels their ancillary lives?

Did your worship falter once you were sure you were good?

How long did you live before yielding to your inevitable shame?

And how long before you realized (did you realize?) shame was a blade

      you turned against yourself

      and once you knew it

                    you could use it—

AWRAH

(Arabic) *nakedness, taboo; that which is prohibited from public view.*

From the root meaning *defectiveness, weakness, imperfection, blemish.*
The word has evolved, in multiple languages, to mean *woman.*

A man who does not know my favorite song opens me like a fig.

He has the proper credentials.
I have a paper sheet
hiked up and my legs spread wide as a wish.

*

My father called it *fig.* Because of this, I avoid eating them for many years, until after I am sick, at which point I begin to seek out any sanguine fruit like kin (as a child, upon first identifying herself in a mirror, begins looking hungrily in any bright pane)—feast on pomegranates, blood oranges, raspberries, cherries, plums. The first time I split the skin to reveal its carmine interior, I blush, I feel I am partaking in something vulgar. Assume implicitly my father meant *shame* but never make certain. But then I taste it. Its red meat on my tongue. Its ineffable sweetness.

*

In the dark, I search an Arabic dictionary for *vagina* by the glow of my phone—touch and touch to keep it from dimming. But it's irrelevant: the word's missing.

Find instead, where it should be: *diamond, suffering, to make a god.*

*

(From the Latin, *sheath.*)

    Sheath

            implies weapon—(whose

            weapon?)—

            implies a weapon

    subdued.

*

It could be cancer, the doctor says, *but you are very young.*

Does young mean less
likely, in this circumstance? I ask.

The doctor is exasperated.
The doctor is an expert
in his field. He sighs

so that I'm aware. I am bare
under paper, a bright bulb. I look down.
My feet touch at the toes like a child's.

*

We're children, we're easily
convinced. Sundays,

Sister teaches us
we are sweet, are sweets,

bonbons, good goods
unless we're unwrapped—

or (heaven
forbid) kissed

—who wants a sucker
that's already been licked?

*

pudendum:

A person's external genital organs, especially
the external genitalia of a woman.

Latin, translated literally as *thing to be ashamed of.*
From the root meaning *to punish.*

*

The idea of disease as punishment yielded the idea that a disease could be
a particularly appropriate and just punishment.

The idea of the disease yielded.

The idea the disease.

*

To the woman He said, "I will greatly multiply Your pain; in pain, your desire will rule over you."
Or this is how I remember it. Some things get damaged when handed down. Some things
get damaged when handled. I am handled by so many men I begin to believe myself a thing,
myself *some thing damaged.* When men tell me things, I listen. It's polite, and I am a woman,

and this a part of the terms. You learn. When the word of God came down it came down to a man. I will not accuse God of lacking imagination, but I will set the accusation down where He can see it. Nevertheless, I take great care to respect the Word, and words generally, the only place I have ever encountered God, thus something of a sanctuary. (Like a child teasing, He refuses to show Himself to me, and so I must keep calling, keep seeking.) I am good, or at least I follow rules. Because I am bleeding, for two years I do not touch the word of God, do not enter His house, do not sing His favorite songs, by which I mean pray. I understand the blood as exile and cry out from the island it makes of me. I cry out in the way I am allowed, which is in puling, plaintive sounds. *Why, O Lord, have you punished me*—et cetera, et cetera. I also distract myself with language, as though I might find God in the lacunae between letters, in the ink of the letters themselves. Pain does not have a language, but God is where, in language, *pain* grew from *punishment* like a woman from a rib. What else can you call it but divine, the way *ill* stems from *evil*'s root, *patient* from *suffering, blessing* and *blood* on the same dark vine—

*

Sister says God
sees all, says God
sees all of us, in every room in every house in every hour we enter, says even in darkness God
sees, in darkness He is the light that illumes, so cover yourself, even when alone, for God
is with you, God
who knows *what your own self whispers to you,* God
closer than your jugular vein.

*

In Arabic, blood becomes *dam,* so with my two tongues I conjure both flood and its obstacle.

*

A poet says *Repent*
means "the pain again."

Sister says *once you touch*
He knows and your hands can never
be clean.

So what do I do with this ache, my filth, and my hands,
stained as they are—my hands
rising instinctive in the morning like birds
wild with impertinent praise?

*

My hair *awrah,* so I covered it.
My skin *awrah,* so I covered it.
The sound of my voice *awrah,* so I swallowed it.
The sound of my feet *awrah,* so I stood so still I vanished, just to be sure.

*

What purpose now, if I was made to worship You and You forbid me worship? I'm anxious as the moon gnawing through a day's haze to be seen. My effort confuses. Praying as a child, I moved as my father moved, my lips contorting into the suggestion of words with nothing said, while in my head, a terrible boredom. As I was taught, tapped my finger against my knee, believed this sanctioned impatience. Now, chastened. Now I ablute and am never clean. I prostrate to pain and think it You. Is it true Maryam stood in worship each day until her ankles swelled as if with pride and her feet festered and wept with blood? I don't understand your distinctions. I've learned the words. Let me put them to use.

*

The doctor speaks to me
as I am told one day a husband might—

I am always supine, undressed,
he is always standing

across the room, impatiently
explaining something. It's a certain kind

of intimacy. We talk briefly
about the usual things—

how I feel,
what he thinks

about his work, which is,
of course, my body. My body the crux

of the relationship.

*

Women, being socialized to attend more to their physical appearance, are more likely than men to have health-care providers assume they are not in pain if they look more physically attractive.

*

And what of looking? If a man looks long enough, a woman becomes something else. A novelty. A gimcrack. And God looks, and His angels, a canary on each shoulder. But this is true of anyone. And the sunbreak searing the clouds is not God's eye. And the rustle outside my bedroom window at dusk is not God peering in. Yet, God watches, unfailing. What does He learn by watching that He does not already know? And what of the doctors' looking? Having looked so long, I think them gods. And anyway, I can't demand they avert their gaze—the looking's what will save me.

*

Pressed, the belly resists.
The doctor pushes again
two fingers—tender. Holds
a golf ball, says, *one's this
size.* Won't say the other.

*

A man saying, once inside, *tell me if
it hurts.*   A man saying *just
a little*

pressure.

*

*Having a tumor generally arouses some feelings of shame. . . Far from revealing anything spiritual,
it reveals that the body is, all too woefully, just the body.*

*

A boy pressing me. A boy pressing me
into the mattress like his shadow. I his
shadow. My body irrelevant. My body
the whole point. My body between us
like an argument, but I uttered no
argument. My limbs shadows, resist-
less. When he moved, I moved with
him. Shadow of a shadow of a boy.
Pressing my head. A boy pressing my

hands above my head. A boy pressing
Come on. A boy pressing *just a little bit.*
Pressing just a little bit on my body,
my hands, my head. Just a little bit of
pressure until met with resistance. Just
a little bit and a little bit and a little bit
more.

*

The disease is often experienced as a form of demonic possession—tumors are "malignant" or "benign," like forces.

*

A little pressure.
A little pressure.
A little pressure.
A little pressure.
A little pressure.
A little pressure.
A little pressure.
A little pressure.

*

A woman writes *Cancer is a demonic pregnancy.* Because life is grotesque
and absurd, the doctor uses a fetal chart to track my tumor's growth;
thus the produce aisle engenders dread. I yield a kumquat within me,
a Meyer lemon, an heirloom purple as a fist. *10 weeks. 13. 20. Your baby
is just beginning to kick. Your baby pandiculating. Your baby, if a girl, has now
eggs and a womb of her own.* I know something grows within me without
eyes, without fingers, a beast without intention or a mouth to speak it,

a creature with no breath blown in. In Arabic, to say *fetus*, ineluctably,

you summon *jinn.*

*

And you, flower of pain, offer me other possibilities, become motherhood.

*

In the Qur'an, when Mary gives
birth, it is not clinical. The sun bearing down on
her like an animal, a thousand
puny suns running
like yolks in globules of sweat.
Beneath her, her bared,
milky thighs and clots
of black sand. This what I cannot
look away from—the One Who Is Most Clean
unclean, her incarmined
hellward crown slicked
as if with lust, her mouth opening to howl
that curse, and a moment where she is
a wretched two-headed creature,
then, after, the offal of God's
will sloughed as if onto an abattoir's floor—
and I stare not to humiliate her but for reassurance
that one can truly suffer, can bleed
and bleed as if gutted
by the blade of God's command,
and still be loved by God
and, more importantly, love Him back.

*

When trying to ascertain a name for my condition—not the illness but
the subsequent obsession with the Mother of Sorrows, *Sanctissima,* Star

of the Sea—I collect words like pearls, roll them over my tongue, relish
the sounds they make, knowing they do not

serve me. *Mariolatry, parthenolatry: worship of the Virgin Mary, of virgins
collectively.* (It's not worship that I feel, wanting to slip into a new skin like slipping

into a bed with fresh, cool sheets.) *Hyperdulia: veneration of the Virgin
Mary as the holiest of creatures.* Broken down, becomes something like *heavenly*

slave. But what I like best is not her adolescent acquiescence
or established chastity, not her being plucked by God's hand

like a daisy from all others in the field, but her overlooked
humanness, her *woman*ness. I probe the image of the Blessed

Mother as often I have dissected pictures of my own, parsing her
as if to possess her, deciding what of hers is

mine. This what interests me: the body, her body
obscured. Emissary

of the feminine, flanked by gods like men and men of God, covered
like a wound. Of her flesh, only her heart, burning,

within view. Cynosure, nonesuch—in the Book
the only woman named, and to be named is to be

defined, corporeal, a beast of worth; she the one bodied
amid a featureless female haze. My adoration

preordained. In the beginning, as a child,
I didn't know she herself was a child, a sister

I would eternally be placed beside—favored girl, exemplar
of the lesser sex—and found lacking. And now a woman, all my life

eclipsed, I cannot bring myself to resent her, ingénue who yielded
to God's impossible request—how could she have uttered anything but *yes*?

*

woman:

9/10 ths of desire.   Man's equal only when she makes   her life a perpetual offering.
       The devil's gateway.   The unsealer of that forbidden   tree. First
             deserter of the divine   law. Tribulation. Hell's   majority. More
shame-   less   and false, more readily   deceived, and more mindful
    of injury, more   watchful, more   idle, on the whole less   excitable.
        A certain lack   of qualities. A misbegotten man.   Defective
and misbegotten.   Weak, typically   sick,   changeable, inconstant.   The relative
        being. Sex,   absolute sex.   Wholly
                in her womb.   A pain
                        that never goes away.

*

Black bag / of desire. Sweet
weight / singing like a school
girl. Chalice. / Teacup. Vessel.
Animal within / an animal. She-
ram. / Bed / of death. *Womb,
black. Blackening, / as a snake you
coil, / and as a serpent / you hiss,
and as a lion you / roar, / and as a
lamb, lie / down.*

*

Two years draped in black trail behind me like a cortege. Suited for a death that didn't come. My prolonged, equivocal mourning. It takes time to be convinced, when I am well, that I am well. I dress in umbrage, as if still under the shadow of a very tall tree. But then I emerge, vernal, into the world of brightness, tentatively allow myself my favorite, imbruable hues—coquelicot, goldenrod, cornflower, lilac. . . And, despite knowing what it's known, my body resumes its efforts toward blooming. When the blood comes, it drops lightly on my gusset like a petal. It is the season of strawberries.

SAINTE-BAUME

Holy Cave

In November, eight months after the surgery, I look out at everything dying and declare it

radiant. He takes my hand on the scarred slope of a mountain

named for Mary—not the mother of our non-savior but His

companion, woman of seven devils and a reputation, one who felt the press of a god's

lips to her. We stand in the gilded shade of beeches, oaks,

leaves falling to our feet like gold shavings, and I am thinking

again of the blood that hasn't come, the expected

blot and this morning's bowl of clean water, my thighs pristine and every tree

from here to horizon sloughing red.

I wonder if it's true, what's said—if Mary, ferried across the sea, carried

a baby adrift in her, birthed the son of the son of God

in a Provençal cave, the walls slicked and its mouth

flooded with light. When we reach it, the grotto tucked in the cliff face

like an eye socket, I sink

into awe beyond language, I swallow its clotted silence. And when I enter

the mountain's belly, descend the steps past soft

leak of limestone and quivering

votive flares, to reach the Rock of Consolation pitted

as a fruit stone and flanked by bronze

plaques, the unspoken names of the unborn carved into their surfaces

as if permanence could bring solace, at the center of the craggy rough-

hewn womb suddenly I am willing

to believe in any god offered, to think this hollow holy,

if it means possible the impossible children—the half deity, the half-beating heart, a fetus

budding in the barren plot—and when I tell him

pray, he sits with me before the simple cross in the dim light

of others' griefs wavering at the altar, we fold

our hands not knowing how, bow our heads, Muslim and atheist fumbling in the dark

chapel of the earth, murmuring, *God of Mary   Mary of God   if   when*

make it so

DELUGE

And behold: I, even I, did bring a flood. And the spirit of God moved upon the face of the waters. And it was said: O heaven, desist! Oh I wish I had died. I'd try on death to find you. I wish sometimes that you were back inside me, in this darkness that grew you. It is a fearful thing to fall into the hands of the living. God filled me as a woman fills a pitcher. God as steep, blue water I vanish into, and leave no shadow. Blue be it: this blue heaven. The little clouds shine in the sky like girls. Are you awake up there? If from so much afar you remember me, send a sign. But to suffer means God is near. (*Astaghfirullah!*) And the silence of God is God. I grew faint when I heard what God was planning; I was too afraid to look. All day the bleeding washed down my sides; at night darkly and helplessly my face, wet. Doom flooded my belly, an old debt. Once again pain and the unsayable, once again world. I carried emptiness in me like a drowned man's mouth. I hurled myself into my grief like a dove, like snow on the dead. Angels don't know whether they're moving among the living or the dead. I still sing to you, almost fatal birds of the soul, knowing what you bring. I heard a voice beating among all that blood: *try to live.* As if there were a God. Why do I worship that which does not hear and does not see and will not benefit me at all? I change in vows, and in devotion. All the limbs of me plead for the ache. I lie down like a sick sheep by the well. I was always emptying and it was all the same wound, the same blood, the same breaking. I've rubies, like the evening. The sea pronounces something, over and over, in a hoarse whisper. The sea keeps rocking in and I want to talk. I am that clumsy human on the shore loving you. *La 'ilaha 'illallah.* Nothing between us except this call, these flashes of lightning, and all that floats. I walk between miracle and confusion. I cannot walk an inch without trying to walk to God, I cannot move a finger without trying to touch God. Oh angels, keep the windows open. I will try hard not to be bad again. I will try hard not to be bad again. God, make me chaste, but not yet. The nakedness of woman is the work of God. I am the lily, gleaming white, upon which God has fixed his gaze. O perfect moon, O fathomless well. Moonlight in the kitchen is a sign of God. Calligraphy of blood on the sheet's pallor. Be merciful when you cause roses to bloom from my blood. Myself the rose, ungodly as a child's shriek. O blessed, silent one, who speaks everywhere—batter my heart. There is only one heart in my body, have mercy on me. Something is in this night, oh Lord, have mercy on me. Aren't you just as tired of the fear within me? I am the tree that trembles and trembles. Undermined by blood, visible to anyone, I run to death, and death meets me as fast. Or, death heard my steps and fled, troubled. Before and after death I loved you, and between I saw nothing but. But we abandon one another. I've abandoned certain angers. I stepped out of my thoughts of death, walking and happily talking and laughing, and breathing. Language of blood like praise all over the body. I escaped from death—or is this the view from the precipice? You must be very close, the grass is shadowless. Look, the trees are turning their own bodies into pillars of light. If I can let you go as trees let go their leaves, so casually, will there be pain? Yes. Will my desires still be unsatisfied? Yes. At the end of the nightmare of knowing, may I emerge, singing. Let me be tricked into believing that by what moves in me I might be saved. I know you, terrible joy, one whose love overcomes me, already with me when I think to call your name. There is still time to say what the two of us never dared. My tongue a dove. Says "infant. . ." Sometimes so quiet I don't know it's there. Mute with desire, I woke trembling. Hush says my drifting blood, cool stardust. My blood alive with voices, made of longing—pieces of cloud dissolved in sunlight. And the water abated, and the matter was ended. I could go back to being who I was. And the angel departed from me.

NOTES

MUBTADIYAH: The Book of Deeds, documented by two angels, is a record of a person's actions, used by God on the Day of Judgment to determine whether the person will enter heaven or hell. Upon the first sign of puberty, the recording begins.

MENORRHAGIA: "True, if I cut it it will bleed, like a can of cherries."—D.H. Lawrence

HYMEN is in conversation with the poem "Ode to the Hymen" by Sharon Olds.

HAEMORRHOISSA is the Greek term used in the New Testament to refer to the "woman with the issue of blood."

ZINA is an Islamic legal term for illicit sexual relations, most commonly referring to fornication or adultery. The Qur'an states, "Nor come nigh to *zina:* for it is a shameful deed and an evil, opening the road to other evils" (17:32).

THE HANDSOME YOUNG DOCTOR, WHO IS VERY CONCERNED and MORCELLATION are written with deep gratitude for Dr. Amy J. Reed for her activism on the dangers of power morcellation. Previously, the risk of the dissemination of uterine sarcoma via morcellation was thought to be 1 in 10,000. After Dr. Reed's activism, the FDA. revised this risk to 1 in 350, and banned the use of power morcellation in the vast majority of uterine fibroid surgeries. Dr. Reed died of uterine sarcoma in 2017.

AWRAH

> In Islam, menstruating women are forbidden to touch the Qur'an, pray, enter the mosque, and have sexual intercourse, among other things.

> "And indeed We have created man, and We know what his own self whispers to him. And We are nearer to him than his jugular vein."—The Holy Qur'an, 50:16

> "Repent means, 'The pain again.'"—Anne Carson, *Nox*

> "The idea of disease as punishment yielded the idea that a disease could be a particularly appropriate and just punishment."—Susan Sontag, *Illness as Metaphor*

In Islam, *awrah* refers to what should be covered or hidden. The most well-known practice of this is the *hijab,* a head-covering that some Muslim women wear to hide their hair in public. Women are expected to cover the majority of their bodies, apart from their hands and feet, in loose clothing. The Qur'an also instructs women to lower their gaze and walk modestly. Some believe *awrah* extends beyond this to include a woman's voice, particularly if a woman is speaking softly, loudly, alluringly, or is singing.

"Women, being socialized to attend more to their physical appearance, are more likely than men to have health-care providers assume they are not in pain if they look more physically attractive." —Diane E. Hoffmann and Anita J. Tarzian "The Girl Who Cried Pain: A Bias Against Women in the Treatment of Pain"

"Having a tumor generally arouses some feelings of shame. . . . Far from revealing anything spiritual, it reveals that the body is, all too woefully, just the body."—Susan Sontag, *Illness as Metaphor*

"Cancer is now in the service of a simplistic view of the world that can turn paranoid. The disease is often experienced as a form of demonic possession—tumors are 'malignant' or 'benign,' like forces—and many terrified cancer patients are disposed to seek out faith healers, to be exorcised."—Susan Sontag, *Illness as Metaphor*

"Cancer is a demonic pregnancy."—Susan Sontag, *Illness as Metaphor*

"And you, flower of pain, offer me other possibilities, become motherhood."—Adonis, "Body"

Mary is the only woman named in the Qur'an.

"God created sexual desire in ten parts; then he gave nine parts to women and one to men."—Imam Ali ibn Abi Talib

"Woman is man's equal only when she makes her life a perpetual offering, as that of man is perpetual action."—Honoré de Balzac, *Béatrix*

"You are the devil's gateway: you are the unsealer of that (forbidden) tree: you are the first deserter of the divine law."—Tertullian, *On the Apparel of Women*

"I have not left behind me any *fitnah* [tribulation/trial/temptation] more harmful to men than women."—the Prophet Muhammad (Peace Be Upon Him)

"I was shown Hell and I have never seen anything more terrifying than it. And I saw that the majority of its people are women."—the Prophet Muhammad (Peace Be Upon Him)

"[The woman] is also more shameless and false, more readily deceived, and more mindful of injury, more watchful, more idle, and on the whole less excitable than the male."—Aristotle, *The History of Animals*

"'The female is a female by virtue of a certain lack of qualities,' said Aristotle; 'we should regard the female nature as afflicted with a natural defectiveness.'"—Simone de Beauvoir, *The Second Sex*

"The female is a misbegotten male."—Aristotle

"As regards the individual nature, woman is defective and misbegotten."—St. Thomas Aquinas

"Finally : woman! One-half of mankind is weak, typically sick, changeable, inconstant— woman needs strength in order to cleave to it; she needs a religion of weakness that glorifies being weak, loving, and being humble as divine."—Friedrich Nietzsche, *The Will to Power*

"It is sad to think that woman, the relative being who can live only as a member of a couple, is often more alone than a man."—Jules Michelet

"And she is simply what man decrees; thus she is called 'the sex,' by which is meant that she appears essentially to the male as a sexual being. For him she is sex—absolute sex, no less." — Julien Benda, *Le rapport d'Uriel*

"But first we must ask: what is a woman? 'Tota mulier in utero', says one, 'woman is a womb'."—Simone de Beauvoir, *The Second Sex*

"Woman is a pain that never goes away."—Menander

"my black bag of desire"—Lucille Clifton, "poem to my uterus"

They said you were sick unto dying
but they were wrong.
You are singing like a school girl.
You are not torn.

89

Sweet weight,

in celebration of the woman I am

and of the soul of the woman I am

and of the central creature and its delight

I sing for you. I dare to live.

> —Anne Sexton, from "In Celebration of My Uterus"

"The womb is like an animal within an animal."—Aretaeus

And when I saw you, in a textbook

of anatomy, full frontal, I saw

a feral unseeing creature, like a she-ram

with great fallopian horns.

> —Sharon Olds, from "Ode to the Female Reproductive System"

"O my accursèd womb, the bed of death!"—William Shakespeare, *Richard III*

"Womb, black. Blackening, as a snake you coil, and as a serpent you hiss, and as a lion you roar, and as a lamb, lie down."—inscription on ancient Byzantine amulets

DELUGE

This poem is made up of lines borrowed from (in order of first appearance): the Bible, the Holy Qur'an, Rainer Maria Rilke, John Donne, Jean Valentine, Carl Phillips, Thomas Merton, Gerard Manley Hopkins, Etel Adnan, Anna Kamienska, Carolyn Forché, Muriel Rukeyser, Anne Sexton, Amina Saïd, Pablo Neruda, Kadia Molodowsky, Lucille Clifton, Emily Dickinson, Annie Dillard, Adonis, Edna St. Vincent Millay, St. Augustine, William Blake, Hildegard of Bingen, Mechtild of Magdeburg, Anne Carson, Mahmoud Darwish, Sylvia Plath, Franz Wright, Paul Celan, George Oppen, Denise Levertov, Nazim Hikmet, Sharon Olds, Louise Glück, Mary Oliver, May Sarton, Alicia Ostriker, Deborah Digges, Jane Kenyon, Chana Bloch, Mary Szybist, Marie Howe, Margaret Atwood, Rumi.

ACKNOWLEDGMENTS

All thanks be to God—I have been greatly blessed.

I am indebted to all the doctors and nurses who cared for me, but especially Dr. Craig J. Sobolewski: thank you.

I am deeply grateful to the organizations and institutions who provided me with the vital time and support to write this book: the Creative Writing Program at North Carolina State University, the Munster Literature Centre, the Quest Writer's Conference, Dickinson House, the Tin House Writers' Workshop, The Frost Place, the Key West Literary Seminar, the Helene Wurlitzer Foundation of New Mexico, the Barbara Deming Memorial Fund, the Fine Arts Work Center in Provincetown, the Wisconsin Institute for Creative Writing, Cleveland State University, and the Anisfield-Wolf Book Awards.

Thank you, Michael Wiegers, for being kind to me when I was first entering this literary world, and for believing in this book all these years later. I am enormously thankful to the entire Copper Canyon Press team for everything they've done for me. It has been a great privilege and joy to work with you.

There would be no book without the endless guidance and encouragement of my many teachers and mentors; in particular Mary Szybist, Joy Harjo, Anita Skeen, Marianne Forman, Stephen Esquith, Joseph Millar, Kim Addonizio, Gregory Pardlo, Sophia Starmack, Caryl Pagel, and Hilary Plum. There are not words enough for my poetry "mama," Dorianne Laux—thank you for everything you've given me, for everything you are.

Thank you, too, to my friends who have taught—and loved—me so much: Emily Rose Cole, Philip Matthews, Tiana Clark, Tia Clark, Oliver Baez Bendorf, Marta Evans, Tyree Daye, Tayler Heuston, Marty Saunders, Dylan Weir, and Rebekah Hewitt. Thank you, Anders Carlson-Wee and Ross White, for your advice and cheerleading. Thank you especially to Rebecca Bornstein, Carlene Kucharczyk, Chelsea Krieg, Laura Thorp, and Allison DeVille for lifting me up during the hardest time.

Michael Deagler, thank you for believing in me, always.

To my best editor, collaborator, friend: thank you for that brain of yours that understands everything, including this brain of mine.

To my family, blood and chosen: all my love.

Bryce Emley, Erin Willie, and Samuel Piccone—your friendship is my greatest blessing and delight.

Henrik—thank you for staying by my side, through all of it.

ABOUT THE AUTHOR

Leila Chatti is a Tunisian-American poet and author of the chapbooks *Ebb* (Akashic Books, 2018) and *Tunsiya/Amrikiya,* the 2017 Editors' Selection from Bull City Press. She is the recipient of scholarships from the Tin House Writers' Workshop, The Frost Place, and the Key West Literary Seminar; grants from the Barbara Deming Memorial Fund and the Helene Wurlitzer Foundation; and fellowships from the Fine Arts Work Center in Provincetown, the Wisconsin Institute for Creative Writing, and Cleveland State University, where she is the inaugural Anisfield-Wolf Fellow in Publishing and Writing. Her poems have received awards from *Ploughshares*' Emerging Writer's Contest, *Narrative*'s 30 Below Contest and its annual poetry contests, the Gregory O'Donoghue International Poetry Prize, and the Academy of American Poets. In 2017, she was shortlisted for the Brunel International African Poetry Prize. She is the consulting poetry editor for the *Raleigh Review* and her work appears in *Narrative, Ploughshares, Tin House, American Poetry Review, Virginia Quarterly Review, Kenyon Review Online,* and elsewhere. She is originally from East Lansing, Michigan, and currently lives in Cleveland, Ohio.

Lannan Literary Selections

For two decades Lannan Foundation has supported the publication and distribution of exceptional literary works. Copper Canyon Press gratefully acknowledges their support.

LANNAN LITERARY SELECTIONS 2020

Mark Bibbins, *13th Balloon*

Victoria Chang, *Obit*

Leila Chatti, *Deluge*

Philip Metres, *Shrapnel Maps*

Natalie Shapero, *Popular Longing*

RECENT LANNAN LITERARY SELECTIONS FROM COPPER CANYON PRESS

Sherwin Bitsui, *Dissolve*

Jericho Brown, *The Tradition*

John Freeman, *Maps*

Jenny George, *The Dream of Reason*

Ha Jin, *A Distant Center*

Deborah Landau, *Soft Targets*

Maurice Manning, *One Man's Dark*

Rachel McKibbens, *blud*

Aimee Nezhukumatathil, *Oceanic*

Camille Rankine, *Incorrect Merciful Impulses*

Paisley Rekdal, *Nightingale*

Natalie Scenters-Zapico, *Lima :: Limón*

Frank Stanford, *What About This: Collected Poems of Frank Stanford*

Ocean Vuong, *Night Sky with Exit Wounds*

C.D. Wright, *Casting Deep Shade*

Javier Zamora, *Unaccompanied*

Matthew Zapruder, *Father's Day*

Ghassan Zaqtan (translated by Fady Joudah), *The Silence That Remains*

Poetry is vital to language and living. Since 1972, Copper Canyon Press has published extraordinary poetry from around the world to engage the imaginations and intellects of readers, writers, booksellers, librarians, teachers, students, and donors.

WE ARE GRATEFUL FOR THE MAJOR SUPPORT PROVIDED BY:

THE PAUL G. ALLEN
FAMILY FOUNDATION

CULTURE

the POINT
envision · enact · evolve

Anonymous

Jill Baker and Jeffrey Bishop

Anne and Geoffrey Barker

Donna and Matt Bellew

Diana Broze

John R. Cahill

The Beatrice R. and Joseph A. Coleman Foundation Inc.

The Currie Family Fund

Laurie and Oskar Eustis

Saramel and Austin Evans

Mimi Gardner Gates

Gull Industries Inc. on behalf of William True

The Trust of Warren A. Gummow

Carolyn and Robert Hedin

Bruce Kahn

Phil Kovacevich and Eric Wechsler

Lakeside Industries Inc.

on behalf of Jeanne Marie Lee

Maureen Lee and Mark Busto

> TO LEARN MORE ABOUT UNDERWRITING
> COPPER CANYON PRESS TITLES,
> PLEASE CALL 360-385-4925 EXT. 103

WE ARE GRATEFUL FOR THE MAJOR SUPPORT PROVIDED BY:

Peter Lewis

Ellie Mathews and Carl Youngmann as The North Press

Larry Mawby

Hank Meijer

Jack Nicholson

Petunia Charitable Fund and adviser Elizabeth Hebert

Gay Phinny

Suzie Rapp and Mark Hamilton

Emily and Dan Raymond

Jill and Bill Ruckelshaus

Cynthia Sears

Kim and Jeff Seely

Dan Waggoner

Randy and Joanie Woods

Barbara and Charles Wright

Caleb Young as C. Young Creative

The dedicated interns and faithful volunteers
of Copper Canyon Press

The Chinese character for poetry is made up of two parts:
"word" and "temple." It also serves as pressmark for
Copper Canyon Press.

The poems are set in Adobe Garamond Pro.
Book design and composition by Phil Kovacevich